25 11/9 7/10   28 X   12·/12 ⁻8 /13   ψ

Skateboarding

Skateboarding

Mike Kennedy

Watts LIBRARY

Franklin Watts
A Division of Scholastic Inc.
New York • Toronto • London • Auckland • Sydney
Mexico City • New Delhi • Hong Kong
Danbury, Connecticut

Note to readers: Definitions for words in **bold** can be found in the Glossary at the back of this book.

Photographs ©: AllSport USA: 51 (Tom Hauck), 45 (Jed Jacobsohn), 50 (Mike Powell), 43 (Jamie Squire); AP/Wide World Photos: 5 left, 16 (Bob Galbraith), 32 (Kent C. Horner); Chris Carnel Photography: 14, 15, 26, 27, 38; Corbis-Bettmann: 22 (John-Marshall Mantel), 52 (Joe McBride), 34, 42 (Timothy Rue), 12, 28 (UPI), 9, 30; Craig Fineman: 2, 5 right, 23, 25, 37; Curt Stevenson: 11; Everett Collection, Inc./Ralph Nelson: 18; FPG International LLC: 20, 21 (Bryan Peterson), 48 (VCG); Mark Richards/ValSurf: 10; oi2.com/Bill Thomas: cover; SportsChrome East/West/Rob Tringali, Jr.: 46; Stone: 6 (Terry Husebye), 33 (Joe McBride).

The cover image shows a skateboarder skating up a half-pipe in Boulder, Colorado. The image opposite the title page shows John Stephenson skateboarding in Marina Del Ray.

Library of Congress Cataloging-in-Publication Data

Kennedy, Mike (Mike William), 1965–
    Skateboarding / Mike Kennedy.
        p. cm.—(Watts library)
    Includes bibliographical references and index.
    ISBN 0-531-13952-2 (lib. bdg.)   0-531-16584-1 (pbk.)
    1. Skateboarding—Juvenile literature. [1. Skateboarding.] I. Title. II. Series.

GV859.8 .K45 2001
796.22—dc21

00-043499

Contents

Skateboarding developed in California when bored surfers began looking for new thrills.

Chapter One

Roll With It

Have you heard the saying, "Necessity is the mother of invention"? It means that a growing need for something often inspires new ideas. That is how the skateboard came to be. It was invented in the 1950s for surfers who wanted a way to ride waves when the ocean was calm.

Thousands of years earlier, still seas were the least of the problems facing the people of Mesopotamia. Around 5500 B.C., they realized they needed a better way to move the immense stone blocks they used to construct their huge palaces and monuments. Their first attempt at making this job easier was a tool called a sledge. (A sledge is a platform that enables workers to drag heavy loads along the ground—sort of like a skateboard without wheels.) The Mesopotamians next discovered that laying a series of logs under the sledge helped them roll it instead of drag it. This was still a tiring job.

About 2,000 years later, the Mesopotamians came up with a new idea: They sliced narrow pieces from the ends of the logs, fastened them to the side of the sledge, and eliminated the heavy logs entirely. The wheel was born!

Sidewalk Surfing

In no time, skateboarders were zooming up **half-pipes** and catching serious air. Right? Wrong. More than 50 centuries passed before the first skateboard was invented. Not that humankind wasn't trying—inventors were always tinkering with clever uses for the wheel. The idea of personal travel was especially exciting. By the mid-1800s, modern versions of bicycles and roller skates first appeared in various places around the globe. Cycling and skating soon became very popular sports. After the invention of the automobile, lots of adults lost interest in cycling and skating. The only people keeping the flame alive were kids.

By the turn of the century, children had begun to build homemade scooters. All you needed was a wooden plank, a fruit crate, and a couple of old roller skates. This hobby was pretty big in California. So was another popular pastime—surfing.

SPRINGFIELD BICYCLE CLUB.

BICYCLE CAMP-EXHIBITION & TOURNAMENT.

SPRINGFIELD, MASS. U.S.A. SEPT. 18.19.20. 1883.

When the waves were suitable for surfing, everyone headed for the beach. When the Pacific Ocean was calm, however, it was a real drag. By the 1950s, surfers were asking themselves an interesting question. Was there a way to surf on dry land? They discovered this was possible by fastening a pair of roller-skate wheels to their surfboards. The first skateboards had arrived!

Cycling and skating became popular sports in the 1800s, as shown by this poster advertising an exciting cycling event in 1883.

9

Who Invented the Skateboard?

No one knows for sure, but many credit Bill Richards. He was raised in California in the 1920s. In some ways, Bill never really grew up. Even as an adult, he loved the feeling of the wind rushing through his hair. One of his favorite sports was surfing. He and his son, Mark, ran a surf shop in California. They had loyal customers who constantly craved the excitement of surfing.

One day in 1958, Bill and Mark thought up a neat idea to occupy surfers when the weather was bad. Father and son sat down in their workshop, sawed off a piece of wood, and then attached roller-skate wheels to it. The novel contraption seemed like it might be fun, so they put it on display in their shop. To this day, many people claim the Richards' creation was the first skateboard.

By 1960, surf shops all over California were selling skateboards. At first, this new craze was called sidewalk surfing. But soon everyone just called it "skateboarding" after the boards themselves. Surf shops everywhere built and sold their own skateboards. Toy companies did the same. The skateboard quickly developed into a fad, as everybody had to own one.

A man named Larry Stevenson, who was good at getting people excited about new ideas, thought skateboarding had great potential. Larry's instinct told him to start his own skateboard company. He founded Makaha Skateboards, and in 1963 decided to sponsor an event where skateboarders could show off their incredible stunts. When word spread, everyone wanted to buy tickets to Larry Stevenson's event. The contest was a huge success. Always thinking big, Larry called the following year's event the National Skateboard Championships. ABC was so intrigued it broadcasted the contest on national television.

Larry Stevenson (left), founder of Makaha Skateboards, helps a young skater perform a handstand on his skateboard.

No Pip Squeak

Brad "Squeak" Blank won Larry Stevenson's first skateboarding contest in 1963.

At about the same time, another young Californian named Hobie Alter was busy starting a company of his own. Hobie made skateboards just as well as Makaha. The two began a friendly competition to see who could design the best boards. They experimented with lighter and more flexible materials. They replaced steel wheels with faster ones molded from clay and hardened by fire. They refined the **trucks** and **axles**, the devices that attach the wheels to the board.

These innovations made skateboarding even more popular. Kids rode their boards everywhere, from driveways to school-yards to city streets. Drained swimming pools were their favorite spots. Since there were no bumps on the surface, the ride was always smooth.

Around this time, American riders such as John Freis, Torger Johnson, Phil Edwards, and Dave Hilton became the sport's big stars. They launched themselves off of specially constructed ramps and spun in the air. They did handstands on their boards, as well as other spectacular stunts that amazed curious onlookers.

How were skateboarders able to keep their balance? Why didn't they fall and hurt themselves? The truth is that many did. In 1965, the American Medical Association said that skateboards were a "medical **menace**." That scared a lot of people, and the sport's popularity began to drop. By 1967, most parents would not permit their children to own a skateboard, and the sport nearly died.

A Nas-Worthy Idea

Frank Nasworthy realized why skateboarders crashed so often. An avid rider himself, he knew clay wheels didn't grip the road well. One day in 1971, a friend told him about a durable material called urethane. Frank, who liked to fiddle around with inventions, thought urethane might work for skateboard wheels. After making a set, he immediately recognized two things: first, urethane wheels rolled more smoothly than clay ones, and, second, they did not slip and slide.

Frank was very excited and showed his discovery to friends. He then started a company making what he called "Cadillac

Wheels." Almost overnight, skateboarding was reborn. Thanks to urethane wheels, the sport was safer and more fun. New skateboard companies popped up everywhere. Different versions of the sport gained popularity as well. People skateboarded down steep hills, maneuvered around obstacles, and thought up creative tricks. A good imagination was a skateboarder's best friend.

At this point, the hardest aspect about skateboarding was finding a place to practice. Skateboarders needed wide open spaces with smooth surfaces. This is when skateboard parks began to appear. The first park opened in Florida in 1976. It

The first skateboard park was built in the late 1970s. Now there are parks in almost every state, including this one in Yuba City, California.

looked like the bottom of a huge swimming pool, with ramps and curves everywhere. For a small fee, skateboarders could ride all day long. The idea was an instant success. Hundreds more opened in the following months. From these skateboard parks came a wave of young and fearless riders. Rodney Mullen became a **freestyle** champion at age 13. Russ Howell introduced gymnastic leaps and maneuvers to the sport. Laura Thornhill became one of the first girls to achieve stardom.

A rider named Willi Winkel also made his mark. His biggest contribution was the invention of the half-pipe in 1977. In skateboarding's early days, generating speed was dif-

ficult. That's why the quarter-pipe, a ramp shaped like half of the letter "U," became useful in the early 1970s. This ramp allowed skateboarders to pick up speed by simply rolling down off of a raised platform. Sometimes, however, Willi liked doing just the opposite. He would gather enough speed on a flat surface, go up a quarter-pipe, and then soar in the air for a moment. Looking at a quarter-pipe one day, he had a brainstorm. Why not move two quarter-pipes together to form a U-shaped ramp? The results were amazing. After

Skateboarder Blaze Blouin performs on the half-pipe at the Pro-Am Championships in Anaheim, California.

charging down one of the quarter-pipes, Willi was able to roar back up the second. This allowed him to fly even higher off the ground.

Soon, riders everywhere learned about the half-pipe and constructed models of their own. The apparatus opened the door to a whole new world of stunts, but it also created a whole new set of problems. Energized by the thrill of catching air, riders adopted fierce skateboarding styles. As the difficulty of their tricks increased, so did the risk of injury. This made it very expensive to run skateboard parks, because families often sued the parks when their kids got hurt. Many parks went out of business. By 1979, for the second time, skateboarding faced an uncertain future.

Hardcore Comeback

In the early 1980s, only a small group of skateboarding enthusiasts remained. But they refused to let their sport die. With fewer skate parks open, riders returned to streets and schoolyards. They kept current with the skateboard scene by reading magazines such as *Thrasher* and *TransWorld Skateboarding*. Meanwhile, the National Skateboard Association was busy organizing contests across the country. Companies such as Airwalk and Vans created lightweight, board-hugging footwear and hip clothing just for riders.

Hardcore riders, including a youngster named Tony Hawk, loved skateboarding's cool fashions and rebellious lifestyle. In 1979, at age 11, Tony told his father that he was giving up all sports, except skateboarding. Three years later, he was

Out-Foxed

After watching *Back to the Future*, you might think Michael J. Fox is an expert skateboarder. That is not entirely true. In the movie, professional riders Bob Schmelzer and Per Welinder performed his most daring stunts. This was certainly lucky for Fox. He once said that he would probably crash if he tried any tricks that hard.

In the movie Back to the Future 2, *Michael J. Fox races to safety on his hover board, a futuristic version of the skateboard.*

crowned national champion. His rise to fame helped create new interest in the sport.

By the mid-1980s, skateboarding had started to enter the **mainstream**. More than 11 million people in the United States participated in the sport, including actor Michael J. Fox. In *Back to the Future*, his character, Marty McFly, was shown "inventing" the skateboard. In the film's sequel, Fox rode a space-age version that had no wheels and was called a "hover board."

Today, skateboarding is no longer just a fad. Companies from around the globe are always improving on boards. They also have created sophisticated safety equipment. Falling still hurts, but at least it no longer means an automatic trip to the emergency room. Riders continually work on amazing new stunts. Skate parks are opening in every state. Skateboarding competitions highlight exciting events such as the Gravity Games and ESPN's X Games. The sport is the subject of hundreds of Web sites. True, skateboarding might not have been an overnight hit. However, centuries after the Mesopotamians invented the wheel and 40 years after Californians began **shredding** on homemade boards, the sport has proven it will be around for a long time to come.

Skateboarders can perform a variety of stunts and tricks with their skateboards.

Chapter Two

Rad Stunts and Tricks

Why do people enjoy skateboarding so much? Some like zooming up the **transition** of a half-pipe and flying off the **lip**. Some like performing in front of crowds, the same way actors do. Some simply like the cool clothes skateboarders wear. Best of all, you can let your imagination run wild when you are on your board. This is how all the best tricks are invented. First, you envision a new stunt in your head. Then, you practice it again and again until you perfect it.

Better Boards, Better Tricks

In the old days, skateboarders were held back by their equipment. They wanted to try different stunts, but their boards would not let them. The first skateboards were much heavier and more rigid than today's models, so it was hard for a rider to do anything really challenging. All that changed thanks to several major breakthroughs.

A crucial one was the use of **fiberglass**. This material was introduced to the sport in 1964 by Larry Gordon. Gordon owned a company that made surfboards, but he was also interested in skateboarding. At that time, everyone used wood to construct the **deck** of a skateboard. Larry knew, however, that fiberglass was more flexible. He soon realized that by combining fiberglass with wood he could build a better skateboard. The result of his work was a deck that bent but did not break. Riders loved Larry's new skateboard because it felt like it was attached to the bottom of their feet.

Another important invention was the **kicktail**. It came late in the 1960s. The kicktail enables skateboarders to lean back and roll comfortably on their rear wheels. Of course, the introduction of urethane wheels was also critical, providing the smoothest ride yet. A smooth ride makes balancing on the board

The kicktail is the back end of the deck that turns up toward the sky. Many of today's boards have kicktails on both ends.

easier and allows skateboarders to attempt more difficult tricks.

A New Bag of Tricks

By the late 1970s, skateboard companies were making much better boards. As you might guess, this is when many of today's cool stunts were invented. Previously, riders mostly imitated the moves they did on their surfboards. Now, they began to develop distinct styles of their own. A new move called the **Ollie** proved the greatest trick of them all.

Before the invention of the half-pipe, riders were limited by the laws of gravity because rising off the ground was difficult. This helped keep skateboarding at a standstill. Then along came a kid named Alan "Ollie" Gelfand. One day in 1977, he began fooling around with a new move. As Gelfand sped up one side of a half-pipe, he transferred his weight backwards and pressed down his right foot on his board's kicktail. The maneuver propelled him and his

Alan "Ollie" Gelfand flies off the lip of a ramp with his skateboard. This trick, later named for him, is the foundation for all of today's stunts.

skateboard into the air—and right onto his rear end! After trying the stunt several more times, he was able to land safely. Skateboarding had taken to the skies. The trick became known as the Ollie in honor of Gelfand.

News of the Ollie spread quickly through the skateboarding world. Gelfand appeared on the cover of *Skateboarder* magazine. He showed other riders how to do his move, and they put their own spins on it. Mark Gonzalez was the first to elevate onto hand rails. Jeff Phillips created the "Phillips 66." Duane Peters, known as the "Master of Disaster," thrilled spectators with the "loop of life." Mike McGill made a name for himself with the "McTwist," spinning backwards on his board one and a half turns in the air. It seemed that somebody added a new twist to the Ollie every day. In fact, riders still dream up funny names for their best tricks. This makes the sport fun, and is another way for skateboarders to be creative.

Getting Technical

Today, skateboarding requires more than a good imagination because the sport has become highly technical. Serious skateboarders practice constantly and leave nothing to chance. They rely on pinpoint accuracy and need full confidence to complete all their stunts during competition.

Skateboarders also realize that they owe a lot to Alan Gelfand. This is because the Ollie remains the basis for nearly every stunt invented. When Bob Burnquist performs his "Burntwist," he is doing an Ollie. When Chet Thomas elevates on a park bench, he is doing an Ollie. When you see a picture of Daewon Song soaring through the air, he is doing an Ollie. As Tony Hawk says, "Almost every trick starts with an Ollie." From there, the skateboarder takes over.

Skateboarding stunts are highly technical and require lots of practice.

The crowded stands at the 1999 X Games in San Francisco is a tribute to the rising popularity of skateboarding.

Chapter Three

Lights, Camera, Action

Skateboarding was not always popular. Back when your parents were kids, only a small number of people were interested in the sport. Competitions were rarely shown on television, and it was hard to find magazines that covered skateboarding. Few people took the sport seriously. They believed that riders would eventually grow bored with it. To make matters worse, some skateboarders had reputations as troublemakers because they didn't always follow the rules in school and at home. This gave critics even more reason to hope the sport would die. Of course, skateboarding did not die, and today it has a following worldwide.

Coming Attractions

There were early signs that skateboarding might be more than a fad. In 1965, *The Quarterly Skateboarder*, the first publication devoted to the sport, hit the newsstands. In May of the same

This 1965 photo of kids showing off on their skateboards demonstrates why some people hoped the sport's popularity would fade.

year, *Life* magazine ran a photo of Pat McGee on its cover. She was the girls' national skateboarding champion. The story inside looked at "the craze and the menace of skateboards."

Around the same time, Hollywood made the first movie about skateboarding, *Skater Dater*, which explored the problem of peer pressure among teenagers. Jan and Dean, a popular two-man singing group, released a song called *Sidewalk Surfing*. The organizers of the National Skateboard Championships in California were also singing a happy tune; suddenly, their event had become a national sensation.

A Healthy Thrash

During the 1970s, skateboarders turned away from the surfer image. In fact, they did not care what people thought of them. Some riders rebelled against society—many had wild haircuts, wore grungy clothes, and used bad language. They believed that no one was ever going to accept skateboarding as a real sport. Little did they know, people were beginning to change their minds.

By 1975, skateboarding contests were popping up all over the world. Despite the "who cares" attitude of many riders, the sport was growing in popularity. So was the number of skateboarding movies being produced. The most famous was *Skateboard*. It starred a teenager named Leif Garrett. He was already a rock star when the movie came out in 1978. Movie critics agreed that the best parts of the film were the skateboarding scenes.

Press Clippings

In 1977, the first articles on skateboarding appeared in *Sports Illustrated*.

Tony Alva is twelve feet above the ground as he soars through the air during this stunt. His skateboarding talents were used in the 1978 movie Skateboard.

This kind of publicity was good news for the sport. Pros Tony Alva and Ellen Oneal performed all of the movie's toughest stunts. Even though *Skateboard* was a dud, at least it helped draw attention to excellent skateboarding technique. In addition, the performances of Alva and Oneal were applauded by hardcore riders everywhere.

These serious skateboarders fueled the sport as it entered the 1980s. They acquired a voice in 1981, when *Thrasher* published its first issue. *Thrasher* took the sport from the streets and put in on the newsstands.

Roll the Cameras

Skateboarding has been featured in plenty of movies, including *Spinnin' Wheels* (1975), *Five Summer Stories—Plus Four* (1975), *Super Session* (1976), *Freewheelin'* (1976), *Hard Waves/Soft Wheels* (1977), and *Police Academy 4: Citizens on Patrol* (1987).

The Big Time

During the 1980s and 1990s, several other magazines surfaced, many of which are still around today. Each offers a different perspective on skateboarding. *TransWorld Skateboarding* features beautiful photography of amazing new tricks. *Heckler* looks at all levels of the sport. *Skateboarder* is aimed at young riders.

The magazine rack is not the only place to learn about skateboarding. For example, two movies released in the 1980s are probably available at your local video store. One, called *Thrashin'*, is highlighted by the awesome moves of Lance Mountain and Chris Cook. The other, *Gleaming the Cube*, is considered a classic. Riders really love this murder mystery because skateboarding legend Stacy Peralta helped direct it. The skateboarding scenes are outrageous, featuring Tony Hawk, Mike McGill, and Rodney Mullen performing some unbelievable stunts.

If you want to see the best skateboarders in person, check out a variety of contests held around the globe. The United Skateboarding Association and World Cup Skateboarding both sponsor events year round. Some of the highlights on the United Skateboarding Association's schedule are the Beast of the East, Skate Jam, and the Grand Prix of Skateboarding. World Cup Skateboarding has a more international flavor, with events like the Vans Triple Crown of Skateboarding, the Alp Challenge in Europe, and the South American Championships.

From Dogtown to the Bones Brigade

Stacy Peralta was a big name in skateboarding long before *Gleaming the Cube.* In fact, he played a leading role on two of the sport's most famous teams. The first was the Z-Boys, which Stacy joined in the early 1970s. Before competitions, the fearsome Z-Boys would boast about their awesome abilities. Then they would go out and prove it. The Z-Boys developed their cocky style in "Dogtown," a rough section of Santa Monica, California. When practicing in Dogtown, the Z-Boys always had to be on the lookout for trouble.

Eventually, the Z-Boys split up. Stacy, however, still hungered for competition. In 1979, he organized the Bones Brigade. It was sponsored by Powell Peralta, a skateboard company that Stacy helped found. The team included Ray "Bones" Rodriguez, Alan Gelfand, Rodney Mullen, and Tony Hawk.

Bob Burnquist performs in the street competition at the 1997 X Games.

Of course, there are also the X Games and the Gravity Games. The X Games, broadcast by ESPN, started in 1995. The Gravity Games began several years later, and are covered by NBC. Both events feature **street** and **vert** skateboarding competitions. In street, competitors wind through a course known as the "funbox," which includes rails, steps and quarter-pipes. Judges score riders based on their technical expertise and the difficulty of their tricks. In the vert category, riders take to the air and try to nail their best stunts on the half-pipe.

The X Games and the Gravity Games attract the top international talent, and the competition gets better each year. Thanks to these events and others like them, skateboarding has truly hit the big time.

Skateboarders who compete in vert events perform stunts on a half-pipe like the one pictured here.

Tony Hawk, shown here rising off a half-pipe, is considered the best skateboarder ever.

Chapter Four

Awesome, Dudes

Skateboarding has produced many great stars over the years. Four of these stand out. Tony Alva was the wildest boarder of the 1970s, Rodney Mullen turned free-style into an art form, and Tony Hawk is regarded as the best ever. Bob Burnquist represents the future of the sport.

Mad Dog

Most people know Tony Alva as "Mad Dog." The nickname suits him perfectly. He was skateboarding's first superstar.

Back in the 1970s, Mad Dog was the leader of the Z-Boys, pioneering an aggressive style of skateboarding that set the tone for many of today's best riders.

Tony spent a lot of time at the beach where he grew up in Santa Monica, California. There, he discovered surfing. Possessing great balance and agility, he was a natural at the sport. He also found that his skills served him well on a skateboard.

Tony first tried skateboarding when he was 8. He was already an accomplished surfer who could perform daring tricks on the waves. His life changed when he realized he could do the same on his skateboard. By age 13, Tony had become one of the nation's top riders. He and his friends roamed the coast of Southern California in search of empty swimming pools to hone their craft. "We were just trying to emulate our favorite Australian surfers," recalls Tony. "They were doing all this crazy stuff that we were still trying to figure out in the water—but on skateboards, we could do it."

In 1975, after graduating from high school, Tony headed for Hawaii. Surfing was still in his blood, and Hawaii boasted the best waves. To make ends meet, Tony modeled for skateboard magazines. He also entered local skateboarding contests. The exposure was great. One day, in fact, a Hollywood producer asked him if he wanted to appear in a new movie, *Skateboard*. Tony was on his way to becoming a star.

That same year, Tony and some friends entered the Bahne-Cadillac Skateboard Championship in California. They found

Tony Alva flies through the air during a skateboarding stunt.

a sponsor, formed their own team, and the Z-Boys were born. The Z-Boys traveled around the world, and no one could beat them. Tony and his friends enjoyed being the best. They dressed in wild clothes, sported radical haircuts, and acted like big shots. "We were pretty hardcore when it came to anybody trying to compete with us," says Tony. "We kind of psyched out everyone before we even started skating against them."

This photo from 1995 shows Tony Alva shredding in a T-shirt from his 1978 movie Skateboard.

In 1977, Tony won the World Pro Championship, the first of his three world titles. Mad Dog loved to experiment with all forms of skateboarding, and once set a world record by jumping over 19 barrels. He liked downhill racing, too.

The business of skateboarding also interested Tony. He started his own company, Alva Products, in 1977. It quickly became known for making some of the coolest boards and accessories around.

Today, Tony is still involved with the sport. Though he has mellowed a bit, Mad Dog has not lost his edge. "The future is limitless," he says. "Skateboarding can take you as far as your mind and body will let you go."

Perfect, Son

In skateboarding, perfection is the ultimate goal. No one knows this better than Rodney Mullen. In a 1986 freestyle contest, he earned his sport's first perfect score. Actually, this came as no real surprise. Rodney is known as the "King of Freestyle."

Rodney grew up in Florida in the 1970s. When he was 11, his family moved to a town called Alachua located in the middle of the state. Rodney was not very happy there. Alachua was far from any towns or cities. "We had a huge piece of property in the middle of nowhere," he recalls. "No close neighbors, just cows."

If nothing else, Rodney had plenty of time to practice skateboarding. He had bought his first board a year earlier. In no time, Rodney developed into a skilled skateboarder, his greatest talent being freestyle. Creative and intelligent, he came up with moves no had ever seen, yet he had no interest in competing. He entered his first contest only after friends tricked him into it. When Rodney won, he realized that competition was fun. He began competing in contests all over the Southeast. Soon, the organizers of these events asked him not to enter because he was too good. Other skateboarders felt they had no chance against him.

Rodney's father wanted him to stop skateboarding, too. He thought his son was wasting his life on the sport and wanted him to start thinking about college. Rodney had always been a strong student. His grade point average rarely dipped below 4.0. Obviously, however, Rodney was also an ace on the skateboard. By the time he entered high school, he was already the national freestyle champion. This created a real conflict for the teenager. Should he listen to his dad and concentrate on his education or follow his heart and pursue skateboarding?

Though Rodney loved skateboarding, he heeded his father's wishes. He quit the sport after high school and enrolled in college. There, he grew depressed because he missed skateboarding. "It was killing me," he remembers. "It pushed me over the edge. I wrote a long letter telling my dad how much I loved him, but that I couldn't live like this."

Rodney headed for California, where he rediscovered the joy of skateboarding. He found that the sport had more to offer than he ever dreamed, including roles in movies. He and a friend started a skateboard company. That company, World Industries, is one of the biggest and most powerful in the industry today.

Rodney is very busy, and does not compete as much anymore. When he does, he enters street events (which have more or less replaced freestyle). Rodney is one of the best street performers in the country, because many of his freestyle moves translate easily to these competitions.

He also has a loyal group of fans. Who is his biggest? His father! "He's really proud," says Rodney. "We don't talk about the old days; we talk about the future."

Simply The Best

Basketball has Michael Jordan. Soccer has Mia Hamm. Skateboarding has Tony Hawk, the "Birdman." There is no debate: Tony is the greatest. "When I skate, I never go halfway," says Tony. "If I don't do my best, it eats at me. It kills me inside."

Hawk developed his killer attitude growing up in Southern California. Born in 1968, he started riding at age 9 after his older brother, Steve, gave him a board. Skateboarding soon became Tony's life. He practiced every day for hours on end. "We had to drag him home," recalls his mother, Nancy. "He would kick and scream."

By 1981, Tony had risen to the top of the sport. For the next 13 years, no one could touch him. Hawk was always a step or two ahead of other skateboarders. He perfected tricks that

Tony Hawk balances with one hand on a rail in mid-air while skateboarding on a half-pipe.

others never thought of trying. During his career, Tony has invented more than 50 stunts.

But even for someone as talented as Tony, it often takes more than natural ability to succeed. That is why he looks to 1988 as an important turning point. Tony had already won eight world championships. In his mind, however, he had not reached his full potential. That changed during an event in Ohio. Up until this contest, Tony skated mostly by instinct. Before competing in Ohio, he practiced the exact tricks he would perform in their exact order. The preparation paid off. He completed all his tricks, including a 720 (two full turns in the air). After that day, Tony took his riding to an even higher level.

Tony Hawk skates the half-pipe at Middletown, Rhode Island.

In 1993, after collecting five more world titles, Tony retired. He had other goals, including raising a family and starting a business. Tony got married in 1996. He and his wife, Erin, have two sons, Reilly and Spencer. Tony also helped found Birdhouse Projects, a company that manufactures skateboards and accessories.

The Birdman was born to fly, however, and in 1995 he came out of retirement. At the X Games that year, he took first place in vert. The best was yet to come, though. In 1999, Tony decided to attempt a 900 at the X Games. No one had ever successfully completed this trick, which requires a rider to spin 2 1/2 times in the air. Tony was primed for the challenge. The huge crowd roared in anticipation. Tony's fellow competitors banged their boards on the ground to get him pumped. He plunged down one side of the half-pipe, back up the other, elevated and turned once, twice and then completed the final half-spin. He landed hard but kept his balance.

Tony had just done the impossible; he had nailed a 900. "This is the best day of my life," he said to his screaming fans. "I couldn't have done it without you. This is the best moment of all time." Every skateboarder, past and present, agrees.

Burn, Baby, Burn

Before the spring of 1995, no one in skateboarding outside of the South American country of Brazil had heard of 18-year-old Bob Burnquist. He was soft-spoken, but he could certainly ride a skateboard. At the Slam City Jam in Canada that year, he blew the competition away with an eye-popping combination of tricks and finished first in the vert ahead of Tony Hawk. Since then, no one has forgotten his performance. Bob recalls, "I never thought I'd place well in the contest. It really didn't sink in until a couple days later. I mean it was awesome."

Bob was born in Brazil in 1976. His father was from the United States, while his mother had lived mostly in South America. They taught Bob and his sister to speak English and Portuguese. By his 10th birthday, he was able to converse in both languages. This was also when Bob discovered skateboarding. Several years earlier, he had tried surfing. Skateboarding seemed like fun, too. "There were about five of us that hung around," Bob remembers. "We shared the same board."

Bob loved growing up in Brazil. He met interesting people, learned

Bob Burnquist catches air during the 1999 X Games in San Francisco.

about other cultures, and participated in all types of sports, including baseball and mountain biking. Bob also honed his skateboarding technique. "Skating the hot concrete ramps and hard-to-skate streets of Brazil gives you an extra edge when you go and skate a perfect ramp," he says.

One talent that Bob cultivated was the switch-stance. This term means a skateboarder can ride with either foot forward. It is extremely difficult to master. For Bob, however, it came naturally. "Being in Brazil helped me not follow the skateboarding norm," he says. "I never had anyone around saying a trick was hard or impossible."

After Bob's big debut in 1995, he began touring around the world. Wherever he skated, competitors marveled at his switch-stance style. In fact, many riders now practice the technique because of Bob. He has plenty of other tricks, too. His most famous is the "Burntwist." "My tricks look spectacular to the outsider's eye, but inside, it's just something I know I can do," he says.

Bob is now an international superstar. Companies pay him to endorse their merchandise. He has his own Web site, where fans can read about him and ask him questions. Bob has become a hero to many, especially in Brazil. "I look at it as a mission to pass on a positive word," he says. "I hope I'm doing a good job."

Most of all, Bob enjoys the simple pleasures of skateboarding. "I just have to skate," he says. "I have to be on my board."

Rain Man

Burnquist is concerned about the environment. One of his goals is to save the rain forests in Brazil.

Skateboarding has led to several extreme sports, such as sand boarding.

Chapter Five

Over the Edge

Good skateboarders are talented athletes blessed with great balance and creativity. They are also fearless competitors who will try almost anything. That is one of the advantages of learning to skateboard. It gives you the confidence to be daring. Here are some of the more extreme sports to which riders have "graduated."

Long and Fast

The two most popular types of skateboarding are vert and street, but there are others. There is a version of the sport called longboarding. The name really says it all. A longboard looks just like a skateboard, but is much longer. Some are as long as 60 inches. The wheels on a longboard are also larger and softer, making for an extremely smooth ride. For this reason, longboarding is probably more similar to surfing. Some surfers, in fact, use a longboard as a training device when they are not on the water.

Downhill is another form of skateboarding. Once again, the name says a lot. In downhill, riders race down steep hills. Along the way, they weave through a variety of turns. The goal is to complete the course as quickly as possible. Downhill was very popular in the 1970s. A rider named John Hutson was probably the best ever. He was known to reach speeds close to 60 mph.

The longboarders shown here are skating down a hill in northern California.

Street luge is another sport that "borrows" from skateboarding. It is very similar to downhill, only riders lie flat on their backs on special sleds with their feet forward. Competitors fly down mountain roads at breakneck speeds, and must wear protective helmets and heavy padding. The sport debuted at the X Games in 1995, and has become one of the event's most exciting competitions. Michael Sherlock is the greatest champion in street luge history. He has won more titles and medals than anyone else.

Snowboarding is a sister sport to skateboarding. This sport first became popular in the early 1970s—many years after the invention of the skateboard. Surfers and skateboarders alike took to snowboarding because it offered many of the same thrills they enjoyed in their sports, including the rush of flying through the air and the freedom to use your imagination. To this day, surfers snowboard to keep fit during the winter. Many of skateboarding's top stars love the sport, too.

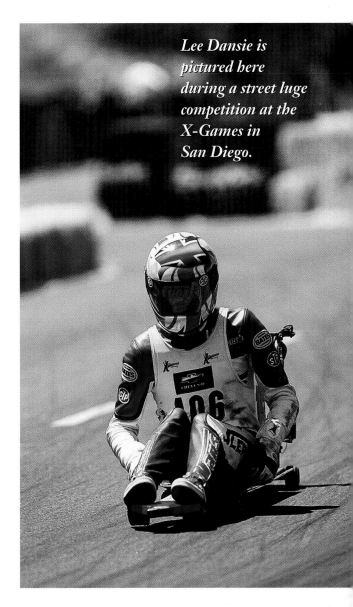

Lee Dansie is pictured here during a street luge competition at the X-Games in San Diego.

Speed Demon

Roger Hickey holds the skateboarding speed record at 78.37 mph (126.12 kph). He set the mark riding flat on his back on a specially designed board.

Sky surfing, a sport that combines skydiving and surfing, is one of the most extreme sports related to skateboarding.

Anyone who has seen someone **sky surfing** one mile above the earth must ask: What's next? The answer is simple: Skateboarders can take their sport anywhere they desire. Who knows? The next Tony Hawk may be living down the street, sitting next to you in class, or even staring back at you in the mirror. As all skateboarders know, if you can imagine it, you can do it.

Timeline

3500 B.C.	The wheel is invented in Mesopotamia.
1850	Cycling and roller skating gain popularity.
1900	Cars capture the imaginations of adults. Kids continue to use bicycles and roller skates.
1958	Bill Richards and his son, Mark, begin making and selling skateboards.
1963	Brad "Squeak" Blank wins the first skateboarding contest.
1964	Fiberglass skateboards are introduced.
1965	The *Quarterly Skateboarder,* the first magazine devoted to skateboarding, debuts. *Life* magazine publishes its first story on skateboarding. *Skater Dater*, the first movie about skateboarding, premieres. The American Medical Association calls skateboards a "medical menace."
1967	Skateboarding's first wave of popularity dies down.
1969	The snowboard is invented.
1971	Frank Nasworthy introduces the first skateboard with urethane wheels.
1975	The Z-Boys compete together for the first time.
1976	The first skate park opens in Florida.

continued next page

Timeline *continued*

1977	Willi Winkel invents the half-pipe. Tony Alva wins his first World Pro Championship. Articles on skateboarding appear in *Sports Illustrated* for the first time. Alan Gelfand invents the Ollie.
1978	The movie *Skateboard* is released.
1979	Skateboarding's second wave of popularity dies down. Stacy Peralta forms the Bones Brigade.
1980	Rodney Mullen is crowned national freestyle champion.
1981	Thrasher publishes its first issue. Tony Hawk wins his first world title.
1985	Marty McFly, played by Michael J. Fox, "invents" the skateboard in *Back to the Future*.
1989	*Gleaming the Cube* is released.
1995	The X Games debut. Tony Hawk comes out of retirement and wins the vert title at the X Games. Bob Burnquist shocks the skateboarding world by winning the Slam City Jam in Vancouver, Canada.
1999	Tony Hawk performs the first 900 at the X Games. The Gravity Games debut.

Glossary

axles—the steel pieces that connect the wheels to the truck

deck—the board minus the wheels, trucks, and axles

fiberglass—a material used to make decks. It is similar to plastic.

freestyle—a type of skateboarding competition in which competitors perform stunts such as handstands and wheelies that are scored by a panel of judges

half-pipe—the U-shaped apparatus on which vert stunts are performed

kicktail—the back end of the deck that turns up toward the sky

lip—the top edge of a half-pipe or quarter-pipe

mainstream—the most popular aspects of a culture

menace—a threat

nose—the narrow front end of the deck

Ollie—a basic stunt in which the rider and board elevate off the ground and onto or over an object

shredding—another term for skateboarding

sky surfing—a sport that combines skydiving and surfing

street—a type of skateboarding competition where riders weave through a course with rails, steps, and quarter-pipes and are judged on the accuracy of their skating and difficulty of their stunts

transition—a change in elevation; the upturn and downturn of a half-pipe are examples

trucks—the pivoting devices that connect the wheels and the axle to the deck

vert—a type of skateboarding competition where riders perform stunts on the half-pipe that are scored by a panel of judges

wheelie—a basic stunt in which the rider balances on the kicktail and rolls forward without the front wheels touching the ground

To Find Out More

Books

Brooke, Michael. *The Concrete Wave*. Los Angeles, CA: Warwick Publishing, 1999.

Cassorla, Albert. *The Ultimate Skateboard Book*. Philadelphia, PA: Running Press, 1988.

Gutman, Bill. *Skateboarding: To the Extreme!* New York, NY: Tom Doherty Associates, 1997.

Jay, Jackson. *Skateboarding Basics*. Mankato, MN: Capstone Press, 1996.

Werner, Doug. *Skateboarder's Start-Up: A Beginner's Guide to Skateboarding*. Chula Vista, CA: Tracks Publishing, 2000.

Organizations and Online Sites

Grand Prix Skateboarding
http://www.gpskateboarding.com
Official site. Includes information on the Alp Challenge held in Europe.

Skateboard Link
http://www.skateboardlink.com
Offers news, photos, profiles and a schedule of contests.

United Skateboarding Association
http://www.unitedskate.com
Official site. Includes information on events, membership, and the "skatepark network." Also offers video clips and "free stuff."

World Cup Skateboarding
http://www.wcs8.com
Official site. Includes information on events, results, and products.

A Note on Sources

In researching this book, I tried to draw on as many sources as possible. First, I consulted with another author named Mark Stewart. He knows a lot about sports, and runs his own company called Team Stewart. Mark pointed me in a couple different directions. Then, I visited my local library and searched its database for books written about skateboarding. The most helpful were *The Concrete Wave* by Michael Brooke, *Skateboarding: To the Extreme!* by Bill Gutman, and *The Ultimate Skateboard Book* by Albert Cassorla. Next, I went to a bookstore to learn about magazines for skateboarders. There were five in all: *Transworld Skateboarding, Thrasher, Heckler, Big Brother*, and *Skateboarder*. I called the editor of each publication for advice and "inside" information. Aaron Meza of *Skateboarder* was particularly cooperative. I also found that *ESPN, The Magazine* had a number of good articles. In addition, many newspapers have published interesting features on skateboarding over the years. Finally, I searched the Internet. There, I discovered scores of great sites, including one devoted to ESPN's X Games. It is worth noting that the folks who run the X Games offered whatever assistance they could.

—*Mike Kennedy*

Index

Numbers in *italics* indicate illustrations.

About the Author

Mike Kennedy is a freelance sportswriter whose work has ranged from Super Bowl coverage to historical research and analysis. He has profiled athletes in virtually every sport, including Peyton Manning, Bernie Williams, and Allen Iverson. He is a graduate of Franklin & Marshall College in Lancaster, PA.

Mike has contributed his expertise to other books by Grolier, such as *Auto Racing: A History of Fast Cars and Fearless Drivers*. The other books he authored in this series are *Roller Hockey* and *Soccer*.